# KUWAIT 2016 HUMAN RIGHTS REPORT

## EXECUTIVE SUMMARY

Kuwait is a constitutional, hereditary emirate ruled by the Al Sabah family. While there is also a democratically elected parliament, the emir holds ultimate authority over most government decisions. The parliamentary elections held on November 26 were generally free and fair with several members of the opposition winning seats.

Civilian authorities maintained effective control over the security forces.

Principal human rights problems included limitations on citizens' ability to choose their government; restrictions on freedom of speech and assembly, especially among foreign workers and a stateless population referred to as "bidoon"; and lack of enforcement of laws protecting labor rights within the foreign worker population, especially in the domestic and unskilled service sectors, resulting in higher risk of human trafficking.

Other human rights problems included reports of limitations on freedom of religion; and restrictions on freedom of movement for certain groups, including foreign workers and bidoon. Kuwaiti and noncitizen women, as well as bidoon and other noncitizens, faced social and legal discrimination. Domestic violence against women remained widespread and unreported, as did violence against domestic workers, all of whom were noncitizens. There were frequent reports of arbitrary arrest and extrajudicial deportation of foreign workers.

The government took steps in some cases to prosecute and punish officials who committed abuses, whether in the security services or elsewhere in the government. Impunity was sometimes a problem in corruption cases.

## Section 1. Respect for the Integrity of the Person, Including Freedom from:

### a. Arbitrary Deprivation of Life and other Unlawful or Politically Motivated Killings

There were no reports that the government or its agents committed arbitrary or unlawful killings.

### b. Disappearance

There were no reports of politically motivated disappearances.

## c. Torture and Other Cruel, Inhuman, or Degrading Treatment or Punishment

The law prohibited torture and ill treatment, although the UN's Committee Against Torture (CAT) during its third periodic review of Kuwait in July expressed concerns about: "consistent reports of torture and ill-treatment in particular during prolonged detention of persons by police and security forces" in cases relating to terrorism and peaceful protests by human rights defenders and members of minority groups. For example, according to Amnesty International, several defendants in the Imam Sadeq mosque bombing in June 2015 stated in court that they had been "tortured or otherwise ill-treated" in pretrial custody, including beatings, electric shocks and placement in stress positions. The UNCAT also cited allegations of insufficient investigation of torture allegations.

Several persons claimed police or Kuwait State Security (KSS) force members beat them at police checkpoints or in detention. In March 2015 authorities arrested a human rights activist, Nawaf al-Hendal, during a protest at al-Erada Square in front of the National Assembly and charged him with slandering the rulers of a neighboring country and for participating in an illegal rally. Media reports stated police arrested and beat al-Hendal and nine other demonstrators. Subsequently, the government imposed a travel ban on al-Hendal. In March al-Hendal stood trial and was acquitted, along with nine other demonstrators, and freed.

The government stated it investigates complaints against police officers resulting in disciplinary action. Disciplinary actions included fines, detention, and some being removed from their positions or termination. Although the government did not make public all the findings of its investigations or all punishments it imposed, it stated it sentenced a police officer in May to two months' detention for sending a noncitizen worker to the detention center without cause. The government, responding to a complaint filed by the worker's mother, investigated the complaint, took disciplinary action against the officer, and ensured the release of the worker form the deportation center. Although the government investigation does not lead to compensation for victims of abuse, the victim can utilize government reports and results of internal disciplinary actions to seek compensation via civil courts.

## Prison and Detention Center Conditions

There were no significant reports regarding prison or detention center conditions that raised human rights concerns.

Physical Conditions:  The Central Prison Complex housed the country's three prisons:  a men's prison for pretrial detention or those convicted of minor offenses, another men's prison for those convicted of more serious crimes, and a women's prison for those in pretrial detention, convicted, or awaiting deportation.  There were approximately 5,400 inmates in the Central Prison.  Cells in the male prison held four to 12 persons and cells in the female prison held four to six; inmates reportedly lived in moderately overcrowded conditions.  There were reports of overcrowding at the women's prison.

A nursery complex was provided for female inmates with children under two years of age.  Officials stated the prison was not designed to facilitate prisoners with disabilities as, by law, any convict with a significant disability cannot be held in the central prison.

There is a separate detention facility for juveniles up to 18 years of age.  The juvenile detention facility contains classroom, vocational workshops, and private meeting rooms for visiting family members.  As of September, the center housed 33 juveniles.

The deportation center at Talha, the only one in the country, housed on average 700 persons.  The overall detainee population was unknown, although observers reported some overcrowding at times and poor sanitation, mostly the consequence of the age of the facility.  Noncitizen women pending deportation were kept at the Central Prison due to lack of segregated facilities at the deportation center.

Administration:  There were no serious problems in the administration of the prison and detention center system although ombudsmen were not available to respond to complaints on behalf of prisoners.

Independent Monitoring:  The Ministry of Interior permitted independent monitoring of prison conditions by some nongovernmental observers and international human rights groups and required written approval for visits by local nongovernmental organizations (NGOs).  Authorities permitted staff from the International Committee of the Red Cross and the UN High Commission for Refugees (UNHCR) to visit the prisons and detention centers.  The government also allowed local NGOs to visit the prison upon approval from the Ministry of Interior.  The Kuwait Society for Human Rights and the Kuwait Association for the Basic Evaluation of Human Rights were allowed to visit prisoners during the year.  A government official stated that approximately 70 local and international NGOs visited prisons during the year.

Improvements:  In September the government opened a special family visiting facility within the prison complex to allow male and female inmates with good behavior records to spend up to 72 hours with visiting family members in a private setting.

**d. Arbitrary Arrest or Detention**

The law prohibits arbitrary arrest and detention.  There were numerous reports, however, that police arbitrarily arrested individuals, principally as part of sustained action against persons in the country illegally.

**Role of the Police and Security Apparatus**

Police have sole responsibility for the enforcement of laws not related to national security, and the KSS oversees national security matters; both are under the purview of civilian authorities at the Ministry of Interior.  The armed forces (land forces, air force, and navy) are responsible for external security and are subordinate to the Ministry of Defense.  The Kuwait National Guard is a separate entity that is responsible for critical infrastructure protection, support for the Ministries of Interior and Defense, and for the maintenance of national readiness. The Kuwait Coast Guard falls under the Ministry of Interior.

Civilian authorities maintained effective control over all security forces, and the government had effective mechanisms to investigate and punish abuse and corruption.

Police were generally effective in carrying out core responsibilities.  There were reports some police stations did not take seriously criminal complaints, especially those of foreigners, and by both citizen and noncitizen victims of rape and domestic violence.  In cases of alleged police abuse, the district chief investigator is responsible for examining abuse allegations and refers cases to the courts for trial.

According to the government, during the first five months of the year, individuals filed 655 complaints against the Ministry of Interior, mostly involving investigative law enforcement personnel.  Complaints included contesting traffic violations, verbal and/or physical maltreatment, and unlawful detentions. Disciplinary action resulted from 201 of the complaints.

Police responded only to the most serious cases of violence between family members, such as spousal and child abuse, and to emergency calls by domestic workers who reported abuse.

**Arrest Procedures and Treatment of Detainees**

A police officer generally must obtain an arrest warrant from a state prosecutor or a judge before making an arrest, except in cases of hot pursuit or observing the commission of a crime. There were numerous reports of police arresting and detaining foreign nationals without a warrant, primarily as part of the government's action against unlawful residents. The courts usually do not accept cases without warrants issued prior to arrests. Authorities generally informed detainees promptly of the charges against them and allowed access to their lawyers and family members.

In July the government amended the national detention laws. Police may hold a suspected criminal at a police station without charge for as long as four days for commission of a felony and up to 48 hours for a misdemeanor, during which time lawyers and family members may visit the defendant upon approval from authorities. During detention, authorities permitted lawyers to attend legal proceedings but did not allow direct contact with their clients. The law provides the detained person the right to a prompt judicial determination about the detention's legality. If authorities file charges, a prosecutor may remand a suspect to detention for an additional 10 days for a misdemeanor and 20 days for a felony. Prosecutors also may obtain court orders for up to six months' detention pending trial by the judge in the case. There is a functioning bail system for defendants awaiting trial. The bar association provides lawyers for indigent defendants; in these cases, defendants do not have the option of choosing which lawyer is assigned to them. There were no reports of suspects being held incommunicado.

The Ministry of Interior investigates misdemeanor charges and refers cases to the misdemeanor courts as appropriate. The undersecretary in the Ministry of Interior is responsible for approving all administrative deportation orders.

Arbitrary Arrest: The law prohibits arbitrary arrest and detention, and the government observed these prohibitions for citizens. There were reports that police during raids arbitrarily detained nonnationals, including some who possessed valid residency permits and visas and who claimed to be bystanders.

<u>Pretrial Detention</u>:  Arbitrary lengthy detention before trial sometimes occurred. Authorities held some detainees beyond the maximum detention period of six months.  Excessive detention in the deportation center, where there are no maximum time limits on detention prior to deportation, was also a problem, particularly when the detainee owed money to a citizen or was a citizen from a country without diplomatic representation in the country to facilitate exit documents.

<u>Detainee's Ability to Challenge Lawfulness of Detention before a Court</u>: Detainees, and those convicted by a court, were able to challenge their detention. In August a prominent bidoon activist convicted of conducting an illegal protest and of assaulting police successfully challenged his detention, resulting in his release pending further adjudication of his case.

## e. Denial of Fair Public Trial

The law and the constitution provide for an independent judiciary, and the government generally respected judicial independence if the judge.  The Supreme Judicial Council nominates all prosecutors and judges and submits nominees to the emir for approval.  Judges who were citizens received lifetime appointments until they reached mandatory retirement age; judges who were noncitizens held one to three year renewable contracts.  The Supreme Judicial Council may remove judges for cause.  Noncitizen residents involved in legal disputes with citizens frequently alleged the courts showed bias in favor of citizens.  While no legal provisions prohibit women from appointment as judges and public prosecutors, the only path to those positions is through work in the prosecutor's office.  In August the Supreme Judicial Council ruled that women prosecutors would be eligible to serve as judges.

Under the law questions of citizenship or residency status and various provisions of immigration law are not subject to judicial review, so noncitizens arrested, for example, for unlawful residency, or those whose lawful residency is canceled due to an arrest, have no access to the courts.  The law subjects noncitizens charged with noncriminal offenses, including some residency and traffic violations, to administrative deportations that cannot be challenged in court; however, noncitizens charged in criminal cases face legal deportations, which can be challenged in court.

## Trial Procedures

The constitution provides for the presumption of innocence and the right to a fair public trial and the judiciary generally enforced this right.  The law forbids physical and psychological abuse of the accused.  Under the law defendants also enjoy the right to be present at their trial, as well as the provision of prompt, detailed information on charges against them.  Criminal trials are public unless a court decides "maintenance of public order" or the "preservation of public morals" necessitate closed proceedings.  The bar association is obligated upon court request to appoint an attorney without charge for indigent defendants in civil, commercial, and criminal cases, and defendants used these services.  Defendants have the right to adequate time and facilities to prepare a defense.  Defendants and their attorneys generally had access to government-held evidence, but the general public did not have access to most court documents.  The Ministry of Justice generally provides defendants with interpreters from the moment charged through all appeals.

Defendants have the right to confront their accusers, to confront witnesses against them, and to present their own witnesses, although authorities did not always allow defendants this opportunity.  Defendants cannot be compelled to testify or confess guilt.  Defendants have the right to appeal verdicts to a higher court, and many persons exercised this right.

Under the new domestic labor law, domestic workers are exempted from litigation fees.  If foreign workers had no legal representation, the public prosecutor arranged for it on their behalf, but with little or no involvement by the workers or their families.  When workers received third-party assistance to bring a case, the cases were often resolved when the employer paid a monetary settlement to avoid a trial.

## Political Prisoners and Detainees

There were several instances of persons detained for their political views.  Throughout the year the government arrested approximately two dozen individuals on charges such as insulting the emir, insulting leaders of neighboring countries, or insulting the judiciary.  Most of those arrested were citizens protesting the Saudi-led coalition's military action in Yemen or criticizing the emir.  Others were bidoons advocating for human rights or opposition political figures alleging government corruption.  While authorities arrested and released some individuals after a few days, they held others for weeks or months pending trial.

In April the government arrested Salem al-Dousari Abu Refa'a for allegedly issuing offensive statements against the emir.  Salem was provided access to legal services, and in November he was sentenced to five years in prison.  The government provided limited access for political prisoners to international human rights or humanitarian organizations.

**Civil Judicial Procedures and Remedies**

The law provides for an independent and impartial judiciary by individuals or organizations in civil matters regarding human rights violations, but authorities occasionally did not enforce rulings for various reasons, including the influence of involved parties or concern for possible political repercussion.  Authorities also occasionally used administrative punishments in civil matters, such as instituting travel bans or deportations.  Individuals were able to appeal adverse domestic court decisions to international human rights bodies if they chose to do so.

**f. Arbitrary or Unlawful Interference with Privacy, Family, Home, or Correspondence**

The constitution and the law prohibit such actions, and there were no reports that the government failed to respect these prohibitions.  Cybercrime agents within the Ministry of Interior regularly monitored publicly accessible social media sites and sought information about owners of accounts, although foreign-owned social media companies denied most requests for information.

Following the bombing of the Imam al-Sadeq mosque in June 2015, authorities required all citizens to transition to an electronic passport.  Citizens were given one year in which to provide a DNA sample at one of the three processing centers.  In July 2015 the government passed a DNA law requiring all persons entering the country, including citizens and noncitizens, to submit DNA samples for security purposes.  Human Rights Watch criticized the law as a violation of privacy, expressed concern over potential misuse of personal information broadly to track individuals.  The United Nations also expressed concern over the "compulsory nature and sweeping scope" of required DNA sampling, and the lack of safeguards and mechanisms for appeal before a court.  In October the emir ordered a review of the DNA law to ensure compliance with the constitution, and in November the emir said that the DNA law would only apply to convicted felons.

The law forbids marriage between Muslim women and non-Muslim men and requires male citizens serving in police or the military to obtain government approval to marry nonnationals.  Nevertheless, the government offered only nonbinding advice on such matters and generally did not prevent marriages between Muslims and non-Muslims.  According to an official, the Ministry of Foreign Affairs prohibited the country's diplomats from marrying noncitizens without the diplomat being asked to resign.

The government may deny a citizenship application by a bidoon resident based on security or criminal violations committed by the individual's family members.  Additionally, if a person loses citizenship, all family members whose status derives from that person also lose their citizenship and all associated rights.

**Section 2. Respect for Civil Liberties, Including:**

**a. Freedom of Speech and Press**

The constitution provides for freedom of speech and press, although these rights were violated.  The courts convicted approximately two dozen individuals for expressing their opinions, particularly on social media.  The law also imposes penalties on persons who create or send "immoral" messages and gives unspecified authorities the power to suspend communication services to individuals on national security grounds.  On September 22, the public prosecutor ordered the arrest and detention for 21 days, under state security charges, of the activist Sara al-Drees for postings she made on social media protesting government actions that suppressed freedom of expression.  She turned herself in on September 25, and on October 6, the Criminal Court released her on bail of 500 dinars ($1,650) pending trial.

Freedom of Speech and Expression:  The 2006 Press and Publications Law establishes topics that are off limits for publication and discussion, and builds on the precedent set by the Penalty Law 16/1960.  Topics banned for publication include religion, in particular Islam; criticizing the emir; insulting members of the judiciary or displaying disdain for the constitution; compromising classified information; insulting an individual or his/her religion; and publishing information that could lead to devaluing of the currency or creating false worries about the economy.  The law mandates jail terms for anyone who "defames religion," and any Muslim citizen or resident may file criminal charges against a person the complainant believes has defamed Islam.  The government generally restricted freedom of speech in instances purportedly related to national security, which included criticism of the emir.  Any citizen may file charges against anyone the citizen believes defamed the ruling family or harmed public morals.

In November, Human Rights Watch published a report highlighting laws that Gulf governments, including Kuwait, use to limit freedom of expression. The accompanying interactive website profiled 140 prominent Gulf-based social and political rights activists, including 44 from Kuwait, who have struggled against government attempts to silence them.

The courts convicted approximately two dozen individuals for insulting the emir, the judiciary, neighboring states, or religion on their social media sites. In April a criminal court found activist Sara al-Drees innocent of contempt of religion charges after she was sued by a group of private citizens when she posted messages about her religious opinions on social media.

In January 2015 charges were filed against MP Abdul Hamid Dashti after he criticized Saudi Arabia's involvement in the conflict in Yemen. Prosecutors released him on bail of 1,000 dinars ($3,300). In July, Dashti was sentenced in absentia to 14 years in prison by the criminal court.

<u>Press and Media Freedoms</u>: Independent media were active and expressed a wide variety of views generally without restriction. All print media were privately owned, although their independence was limited. The government did not permit non-Islamic religious publishing companies, although several churches published religious materials solely for their congregations' use. The law allows for large fines and up to 10 years in prison for persons who use any means (including media) to subvert the emiri system of government. The Ministry of Commerce and Industry may ban any media organization at the request of the Ministry of Information. Media organizations can challenge media bans in the administrative courts. Newspaper publishers must obtain an operating license from the Ministry of Information. In October the government banned media coverage of tribal caucuses in order to enforce the law from 1996 banning them.

Broadcast media are a mix of government and privately owned stations, subject to the same laws as print media.

Before the annual international book fair held in November, the Ministry of Information requires publishers to submit a list of books they might offer at the event. Censor officers at the Ministry of Information review books to determine if content is appropriate. If an officer determines that a book should be censored, the book is referred to a censor committee consisting of 9 to 10 members who determine the appropriateness of the book. The author can appeal the censor committee findings to an appeals committee comprising four to five members. If the appeals committee upholds the censoring, the author has final recourse to appeal the finding in the courts.  Members of both committees are selected by the under secretary and assistant under secretaries on an annual basis and also includes members of the academic community and members of the writers guild.  In November the government added more than 100 books to a list of banned books, including the book *Smile* due to its depiction of gender integration.  Most of the books on the banned list revolved around religion, politics, and public morality.

Throughout the year publishers reportedly received pressure from the Ministry of Information, resulting in the publishers often restricting which books are made available in the country.  According to the Ministry of Information, the Ministry of Awqaf and Islamic Affairs reviewed books religious in nature.  The government did not impose additional restrictions on online newspapers or journals.

Censorship or Content Restrictions:  The Ministry of Information censored all imported books, commercial films, periodicals, videotapes, CDs, DVDs, and other materials deemed illegal per the guidelines enumerated for speech and media.  Media outlets exhibited a range of opinions on topics relating to social problems, but most self-censored, avoiding critical discussion on topics like the emir, foreign policy, and religion, to avoid criminal charges or fines or to keep their licenses.  Discussions of certain social topics, such as the role of women in society and sex were also self-censored.  Authorities censored most English-language educational materials that mentioned the Holocaust and required education material either to refer to Israel as "Occupied Palestine" or to remove such references, although authorities did not censor these topics in news media.  Widely available satellite dishes and virtual private networks allowed unfiltered media access.

National Security:  The law forbids publication or transmission of any information deemed subversive to the constitutional system on national security grounds.  The government prosecuted online bloggers and social media outlets under the new cybercrime law, the Printing and Publishing Law, and the National Security Law.

**Internet Freedom**

In July 2015 the government passed a cybercrime law that criminalizes online activity to include illegal access to IT systems; unauthorized access to confidential information; blackmail; use of the internet for terrorist activity; money laundering; and utilizing the internet for human trafficking.  The law was implemented in January with the publishing of the law in the *National Gazette*.  Fines ranged from

3,000 dinars ($9,900) and a three-year prison term for online blackmail to 50,000 dinars ($165,000) and a 10-year prison sentence for money laundering.

The government monitored internet communications, such as blogs and discussion groups, for defamation and generalized security reasons. The Ministry of Communications continued to block websites considered to "incite terrorism and instability" and required internet service providers to block websites that "violate [the country's] customs and traditions." The government prosecuted and punished individuals for the expression of political or religious views via the internet, including by e-mail and social media, based on existing laws related to libel, national unity, and national security. The government prosecuted some online bloggers under the 2006 Printing and Publishing Law and the National Security Law.

In July the government implemented the Electronic Media Law that establishes regulations and oversight for online commercial and private internet websites and activities. The law requires individuals to procure a license to establish internet sites and businesses and identifies the Ministry of Information as the regulatory body. The law states an individual must be at least 21 years old to apply for a license. As of September the government had issued 148 licenses with 126 applications pending.

The government filtered the internet to block pornography primarily, as well as lesbian, gay, bisexual, transgender, and intersex (LGBTI) material, some secular sites, and sites critical of Islam.

The country had a high internet penetration rate due in large part to pervasive ownership of smart phones. The World Bank reported an internet penetration rate of 82 percent.

**Academic Freedom and Cultural Events**

The law provides for the freedoms of opinion and research, but self-censorship limited academic freedom, and the law prohibits academics from criticizing the emir or Islam.

The Ministry of Interior reserved the right to approve or reject public events and those it considered politically or morally inappropriate.

**b. Freedom of Peaceful Assembly and Association**

## Freedom of Assembly

The constitution provides for freedom of assembly, but the government restricted this right in the case of noncitizens. The law prohibiting them from demonstrating or protesting.

Officials sometimes also restricted the location of planned protests to designated public spaces, citing public safety and traffic concerns. Courts tried and sentenced participants in unlicensed demonstrations to as many as two years in prison for their involvement, and authorities also administratively deported dozens of noncitizens for participation in rallies.

## Freedom of Association

The constitution provides for freedom of association, but the government restricted this right. The law prohibits officially registered groups from engaging in political activities.

The government used its power to register associations as a means of political influence. The Ministry of Social Affairs and Labor can also reject an NGO's application if it deems the NGO does not provide a public service. There were approximately 120 officially licensed NGOs in the country, including a bar association, other professional groups, and scientific bodies. Dozens of unlicensed civic groups, clubs, and unofficial NGOs had no legal status, and many of those chose not to register due to bureaucratic inconvenience or inability to meet the minimum 50-member threshold. The Ministry of Social Affairs and Labor rejected some license requests, contending established NGOs already provided services similar to those the petitioners proposed. Members of licensed NGOs must obtain permission from the ministry to attend international conferences as official representatives of their organization.

## c. Freedom of Religion

See the Department of State's *International Religious Freedom Report* at www.state.gov/religiousfreedomreport/.

## d. Freedom of Movement, Internally Displaced Persons, Protection of Refugees, and Stateless Persons

The constitution generally provides for freedom of internal movement, but numerous laws constrain foreign travel.

The government generally cooperated with UNHCR and other humanitarian organizations in providing protection and assistance to refugees, returning refugees, asylum seekers, stateless persons, or other individuals of concern.

Foreign Travel:  Bidoon and foreign workers faced problems with, or restrictions on, foreign travel.  The government restricted the ability of some bidoon to travel abroad by not issuing travel documents, although it permitted some bidoon to travel overseas for medical treatment and education, and to visit Saudi Arabia for the annual Hajj (Islamic pilgrimage).  The Ministry of Interior has not issued "Article 17" passports (temporary travel documents that do not confer nationality) to bidoon except on humanitarian grounds since 2014.

The law also permits travel bans on citizens and nonnationals accused or suspected of violating the law, including nonpayment of debts, and it allows other citizens to petition authorities to impose one.  This provision resulted in delays and difficulties for citizens and foreigners leaving the country.  Numerous domestic workers who escaped from abusive employers reported waiting several months to regain passports, which employers illegally took from them when they began their employment.

Exile:  While the constitution prohibits exile of citizens, the government can deport foreigners for a number of legal infractions.  While the constitution states the "emir is the head of state and shall be immune and inviolable," it also states, "No Kuwaiti may be deported from Kuwait."

Citizenship:  By law the government is prohibited from revoking the citizenship of an individual who is born a citizen unless that individual has obtained a second nationality, which is against the law.  Nevertheless, the government can revoke the citizenship of naturalized citizens for cause, including a felony conviction, and subsequently deport them.  During 2014 the government revoked the citizenship of at least 33 individuals--some dual nationals, some not--including opposition activists, a media owner, a Salafist cleric, and several tribal members.  The government justified the revocations by citing a 1959 nationality law that permits withdrawal of citizenship from naturalized Kuwaitis who acquired citizenship dishonestly or threatened to "undermine the economic or social structure of the country."  Additionally, if a person loses citizenship, all family members whose status derives from that person also lose their citizenship and all associated rights.

In April the Court of Cassation scheduled a hearing to consider the legality of the revocation of citizenship of former MP Abdullah al-Barghash and his family (al-Barghash was one of the 33 who had his citizenship revoked in 2014). In May the court suspended dealing with the case until a request for a new judge could be resolved. In October an administrative court restored citizenship to Ahmad Jabr al-Shemmari, the former owner of opposition media Alam al-Youm newspaper and television station, after the Court of Cassation ruled that the courts had jurisdiction over citizen revocation cases. Persons who had their citizenship revoked, and any family members dependent on that individual for their citizenship status, became stateless individuals. Authorities can seize the passports and civil identification cards of persons who lose their citizenship and enter a "block" on their names in government databases. This "block" prevented former citizens from traveling or accessing health care and other government services reserved for citizens. There were no known revocations of citizenship during the year.

The law prohibits the granting of citizenship to non-Muslims, but it allows non-Muslim male citizens to transmit citizenship to their descendants. According to the law, children derive citizenship solely from the father; children born to citizen mothers and nonnational fathers do not inherit citizenship. Female citizens may sponsor their nonnational children (regardless of age) and husbands for residency permits, and they may petition for naturalization for their children if the mother becomes divorced or widowed from a noncitizen husband.

**Protection of Refugees**

<u>Access to Asylum</u>: The law does not provide for granting asylum or refugee status. There is no system for providing protection to refugees, and the government did not grant refugee status or asylum during the year. According to UNHCR, there were more than 3,000 registered asylum seekers and recognized refugees in the country. Most of these were from Syria, Iraq, and Somalia, and many were either employed with access to basic services or supported by human rights groups pending resolution of their asylum request.

**Stateless Persons**

The law does not provide noncitizens, including bidoon, a clear or defined opportunity to gain nationality. The judicial system's lack of authority to rule on the status of stateless persons further complicated the process for obtaining citizenship, leaving bidoon with no access to the judiciary to present evidence and plead their case for citizenship. According to government figures, there were approximately 96,000 bidoon in the country, while Human Rights Watch estimated the bidoon population at more than 105,000.

The naturalization process for bidoon is not transparent, and decisions appeared arbitrary.  As of April the Central Agency had more than 96,000 bidoon citizenship requests under review.

According to bidoon activists and government officials, many bidoon were unable to provide documentation proving ties to the country sufficient to qualify for citizenship.  The government alleged that the vast majority of bidoon concealed their "true" nationalities and were not actually stateless.  According to the government, as of September, 8,004 bidoon have adjusted their legal status since 2011 claiming Saudi, Iraqi, Syrian, Iranian, Jordanian, and other nationalities.  In April the government stated that 32,000 bidoon were qualified for consideration for citizenship but that only 8,000 would be eligible due to their security status and criminal records.

According to UNHCR, some bidoon underwent DNA testing to prove their Kuwaiti nationality.  Bidoon are required to submit DNA samples confirming paternity in order to become naturalized, a practice critics said leaves them vulnerable to denial of citizenship based on genealogical bias.

The government discriminated against bidoon in some areas.  Some bidoon and international NGOs reported that the government did not uniformly grant some government services and subsidies to bidoon, including education, employment, medical care, and the issuance of civil documents, such as birth, marriage, and death certificates.  Bidoon activists claimed many bidoon families were unable to obtain birth certificates for their children, which restricted the children's ability to obtain government-issued identification cards, access adequate medical care, and attend school.

According to a government official, the government issued 2,664 birth and death certificates to bidoon in the first nine months of 2015.  The Ministry of Justice issued 1,439 marriage and divorce certificates to bidoon in the first nine months of 2015.  But government sources stated approximately 15,000 bidoon children were not provided birth certificates due to security restrictions.  The Ministry of Education partners with the Charity Fund for Education to pay for bidoon children to attend private schools, but the children must fall into one of seven categories to qualify for an education grant.  According to government officials, as of May, 510 bidoon students were attending Kuwait University.

Zakat House, a government agency that falls under the Religious Affairs Directorate, collected and dispensed donations, provided food, subsidies, financial aid, and training to bidoon and provided monthly financial assistance to 14,455 bidoon families totaling 6.5 million dinars ($21.45 million) from January through June. It also paid for the DNA testing required for every bidoon applying for citizenship.

Many adult bidoon also lacked identification cards, preventing them from engaging in lawful employment or obtaining travel documents. This restriction resulted in some bidoon children from the household working as street vendors to help support their families and not receiving an education. Many bidoon children who attended school enrolled in substandard private institutions because only citizens may attend public school. In May 2015, however, the government approved the transfer of 5,000 bidoon students from private to public schools due to their families' service in the military. Many bidoon families depended on charity to assist with medical and educational expenses. The government announced it issued 35,844 identification cards to Bidoon as of May.

The government allowed bidoon to work in some government positions, as dictated in the 2011 decree, including in the military. In March the government announced there were 2,030 bidoon, who were children of Kuwaiti mothers, in the army.

Since the government treats them as illegal immigrants, bidoon do not have property rights.

In 2014 a high-level official in the Ministry of Interior announced a proposal to give "economic citizenship" of the small island country of Comoros to the bidoon. At the time rights groups were concerned that the government might force them to take another, illegitimate nationality and potentially be vulnerable to deportation. As of September, the Comoros plan remained under deliberation.

## Section 3. Freedom to Participate in the Political Process

Citizens had only limited, indirect control of the executive branch because the constitution stipulates the country is a hereditary emirate. The 50 elected members of the National Assembly (along with government-appointed ministers) must, by majority vote based on universal and equal suffrage and conducted by secret ballot guaranteeing the free expression and the will of the people, approve the emir's choice of crown prince (the future emir). The crown prince must be a male descendant of Sheikh Mubarak Al Sabah and meet three additional requirements: have attained the age of majority, possess a sound mind, and be a legitimate son of Muslim parents.  The National Assembly may remove the emir from power by a two-thirds majority vote if it finds that any of these three conditions is or was not met.

**Elections and Political Participation**

Recent Elections:  Observers generally considered the 2016 parliamentary election free and fair and found no serious procedural problems.  The election followed the emir's October 2016 order to dissolve the National Assembly because of "mounting security challenges and volatile regional developments."  Most opposition politicians and their supporters who boycotted the 2013 election returned and participated without incident.  Official turnout for the 2016 elections was approximately 70 percent.

Political Parties and Political Participation:  The government did not recognize any political parties or allow their formation, although no formal law bans political parties.  National Assembly candidates must nominate themselves as individuals.  Well-organized, unofficial blocs operated as political groupings, and MPs formed loose alliances.  Some tribes held illegal primaries to maximize their members' chances for election to the National Assembly.  In June the National Assembly amended the election law to bar those convicted of insulting the emir and Islam from running for elected office.  Voters register to vote every February upon reaching voting age of 21.  Prosecutors and judges from the Ministry of Justice supervise election stations.  Women prosecutors served as supervisors for the first time during the 2016 elections.

Participation of Women and Minorities:  Although women gained the right to vote in 2005, they still faced cultural and social barriers to political participation.  For example, some tribal leaders excluded women from tribal primaries.  In the 2016 elections, 15 women filed candidate application.  One candidate withdrew resulting in 14 women standing for election with one woman successfully winning a seat.  Women voted at a higher rate than men.

No laws or cultural practices prevented minorities from participating in political life.  In the 2016 parliamentary elections, candidates from the Shia community, which comprised approximately one-third of the citizen population, won six seats in parliament.

## Section 4. Corruption and Lack of Transparency in Government

The law mandates criminal penalties for corruption by government officials, but the government did not implement the law effectively. Government observers believed officials engaged in corrupt practices with impunity. There were numerous reports of government corruption during the year.

There were many reports that individuals had to pay intermediaries to receive routine government services. Police corruption was a problem, especially when one party to a dispute had a personal relationship with a police official involved in a case. Widespread reports indicated that police favored citizens over noncitizens. There were several reports of corruption in the procurement and bidding processes for lucrative government contracts.

All judicial officers received training on corruption and transparency obligations as part of the Judicial Institute's official curriculum.

Corruption: The Audit Bureau is an agency responsible for supervising public expenses and revenues and for preventing any misuse or manipulation of public funds. The government distributes reports by the Audit Bureau annually to the emir, prime minister, head of parliament, and minister of finance. The public did not have access to these reports. The parliamentary Committee on the Protection of Public Funds frequently announced inquiries into suspected misuse of public funds, but none resulted in prosecution during the year.

A 2012 law establishing an Anti-Corruption Authority (ACA) was overturned by the Constitutional Court in 2015 because the law was based on emergency decree. In January the National Assembly passed a new draft bill to re-establish the ACA, which was implemented in November. The law charges the ACA with receiving and analyzing complaints and forwarding complaints to the appropriate authorities in either the Public Prosecutor's Office or police for further investigation or action.

Media and government officials reported cases of widespread, visa-related corruption, namely selling visas or visa fraud, at the Ministry of Social Affairs and Labor and Ministry of Interior. Several officials at the Ministry of Interior faced prosecution after their arrests on charges of falsifying labor import documents to profit from the sale of visas. In October 2015 media reported the government ordered the arrest of a key visa trafficker who recruited 1,500 foreign workers on fake work permits.

In September 2015 the minister of electricity, water, and public works resigned after his conviction, along with 14 other officials, in a corruption case dating to 2007.  The group was later acquitted in an appeals court decision, and the minister was reappointed in February.

Financial Disclosure:  In November government officials began filing financial disclosure statements with the ACA after the law came into effect.

Public Access to Information:  The law provides for public access to unclassified government information by citizens and noncitizens alike.  Unclassified information was available through requests to the relevant government ministry, and the government was responsive to requests.

**Section 5. Governmental Attitude Regarding International and Nongovernmental Investigation of Alleged Violations of Human Rights**

The government imposed some limits on the operations of domestic and international human rights groups.  A number of domestic and international human rights groups generally operated with limited restrictions, investigating and publishing their findings on human rights cases.  The law permits the existence of NGOs, but the government continued to deny registration to some.  NGOs may not engage in political activity or encourage sectarianism.  Officially registered groups must demonstrate that their existence is in the public interest.  Official NGOs must show they will conduct business beneficial to the country; their work cannot undermine cultural values and norms as defined by the government.  Major local independent NGOs dedicated specifically to human rights included the Kuwait Human Rights Society and the Kuwaiti Society for Fundamental Human Rights. The Kuwait Trade Union Federation was the local affiliate of the Solidarity Center. In May 2015 the government closed the chapter of Transparency International, accusing the NGO of exaggerating the level of corruption in the country.

Locally licensed NGOs devoted to the rights or welfare of specific groups--such as women, children, prisoners, and persons with disabilities--operated with little government interference, as did a few dozen local, unregistered human rights groups.  The government and various National Assembly committees met occasionally with local NGOs and generally responded to their inquiries.

Government Human Rights Bodies:  The National Assembly's Human Rights Committee, which operated independently of the government, is an advisory body that primarily hears individual complaints of human rights abuses.  The committee visited the Central Prison and the central deportation center throughout the year to review overcrowding, prison and detainee treatment, and the condition of both facilities.  The committee had adequate resources and was considered effective.  It did not issue reports during the year.  In December 2015 the Ministry of Foreign Affairs established an office of human rights funded by and under the authority of the ministry's legal department.  The office's purpose is to produce human rights reports and respond to such reports produced by international organizations and governments that reference Kuwait.

## Section 6. Discrimination, Societal Abuses, and Trafficking in Persons

### Women

Rape and Domestic Violence:  Rape carries a maximum penalty of death, which the courts occasionally imposed for the crime; spousal rape is not a crime.  Authorities did not effectively enforce laws against rape.  Violence against women continued to be a problem.  There were reports alleging that some police stations did not take seriously reports by both citizens and noncitizens of rape and domestic violence.

Media reported two to three dozen rape cases, but government statistics were unavailable.  Incidents of rape were likely underreported to authorities due to intense social stigma associated with sexual violence crimes.  Many victims were noncitizen domestic workers.  When reported, police typically arrested and investigated alleged rapists and, in a limited number of cases, prosecuted the accused.  In September 2015 the Court of Cassation revoked a life sentence on a citizen for raping a Filipina woman and instead sentenced him to death.

The government does not publish statistics on violence against women.  A local women's advocacy NGO estimated 20,000 women were victims of some form of domestic violence or abuse during the year.  The law does not specifically prohibit domestic violence, but in some instances courts try such cases as assault.  A victim of domestic violence may file a complaint with police requesting formal charges be brought against the alleged abuser.  Victims, however, did not report most domestic abuse cases, especially outside the capital.  There were no known shelters specifically for victims of domestic violence.  In July 2015 the government established two hotlines for reporting domestic violence.  The hotlines are operational only during the working hours and are operated by staff with limited training.  Calls and cases are referred to professional social workers.  In some cases hospitals denied treatment for victims of sexual assault who had not reported the case to the police first.  In December 2015 a noncitizen woman who was raped sought medical care at a hospital but was informed that a police officer would have to interview her first.

A woman may petition for divorce based on injury from spousal abuse, but the law does not provide a clear legal standard regarding what constitutes injury. Additionally, a woman must provide at least two male witnesses (or a male witness and two female witnesses) to attest to such injury.

Other Harmful Traditional Practices:  Officials did not report any honor killings during the year.  The penal code penalizes some honor crimes as misdemeanors. The law states that a man who sees his wife, daughter, mother, or sister in the "act of adultery" and immediately kills her or the man with whom she is committing adultery faces a maximum punishment of three years' imprisonment and a fine of 225 dinars ($743).

Sexual Harassment:  Human rights groups characterized sexual harassment in the workplace as a pervasive and unreported problem.  No specific law addresses sexual harassment, but the law criminalizes "encroachment on honor," which encompasses everything from touching a woman against her will to rape, and police strictly enforced this law.  The government deployed female police officers specifically to combat sexual harassment in shopping malls and other public spaces.  Perpetrators of sexual harassment and assault faced fines and imprisonment.

Reproductive Rights:  There were no reports of government interference in the right of couples and individuals to decide freely the number, spacing, and timing of children; to manage their reproductive health; and to have access to the information and means to do so free from discrimination, coercion, and violence. The information and means to make decisions, as well as skilled attendance during prenatal care, essential obstetric care, childbirth, and postpartum care were freely available.  While the government did not provide any formal family planning programs, contraceptives were available without prescription to citizens and noncitizens:  44 percent of women ages 15-49 used a modern type of contraceptives, and 16 percent of women had an unmet need for family planning, according to UN Population Fund 2015 estimates.

Discrimination:  Women do not enjoy the same legal status and rights as men, but citizen women enjoyed many political rights, including the right to vote and to serve in parliament and the cabinet (see section 3, Elections and Political

Participation).  Sharia (Islamic law) courts have jurisdiction over personal status and family law cases for Sunni and Shia Muslims.  Sharia, as implemented in the country, discriminates against women in judicial proceedings, freedom of movement, marriage, child custody, and inheritance.  There were no known cases of official or private-sector discrimination in, credit, owning and/or managing a business, and housing.  Discrimination in employment and occupation occurred with respect to both citizen and noncitizen women.  Secular courts allow any person to testify and consider male and female testimony equally, but in sharia courts, which govern personal status matters such as marriage, divorce, child custody and inheritance issues, the testimony of one man equals that of two women.

The 1984 Kuwaiti Family Law Code prohibits marriage between Muslim women and non-Muslim men.  The law does not require a non-Muslim woman to convert to Islam to marry a Muslim man, but many non-Muslim women faced strong economic and societal pressure to convert.  In the event of a divorce, the law grants the father or his family sole custody of children of non-Muslim women who do not convert.  A non-Muslim woman who does not convert to the religion of her husband is also ineligible for naturalization as a citizen and cannot inherit her husband's property unless specified as a beneficiary in his will.

Inheritance is also governed by sharia, which varies according to the specific school of Islamic jurisprudence.  In the absence of a direct male heir, a Shia woman may inherit all property, while a Sunni woman inherits only a portion, with the balance divided among brothers, uncles, and male cousins of the deceased.

Female citizens are unable to pass citizenship to their noncitizen husbands or their children; however, exceptions were made for some children of widowed or divorced female citizens (see section 2.d., Stateless Persons).  In August the government awarded citizenship to 180 children of Kuwaiti widows and divorcees.  Male citizens married to female noncitizens do not face such discrimination.  In May parliament approved awarding loans up to 70,000 dinars ($231,000) for single Kuwaiti women.  The law grants a "housewife allowance" to nonworking women age 55 and older.

Women experienced discrimination in the workplace (see section 7.d.).

According to government statistics, women comprised only 14 percent of legislators, senior officials, and managers.

In October the country's highest court ordered an end to affirmative action for male applicants to medical schools on grounds it is unconstitutional.  Prior to this court ruling, female applicants were required to demonstrate a higher minimum grade point average than male applicants.  The law requires segregation by gender of classes at all universities and secondary schools, although it was not always enforced.

A limited number of women attained leadership positions in the private sector as heads of corporations, but only one woman served as a minister in the cabinet.

In 2014 the first 22 female employees of the Public Prosecutor's Office completed their training and became public prosecutors, a prerequisite for appointment as a judge.  In August the Supreme Judicial Council ruled that after serving as prosecutors for three years women would be eligible to serve as judges.

**Children**

Birth Registration:  Citizenship derives entirely from the father; children born to citizen mothers and noncitizen fathers do not inherit Kuwaiti citizenship unless the mother is divorced or widowed from the noncitizen father and may then facilitate the child's application for citizenship.  The government designates religion on birth and marriage certificates.  The government often granted citizenship to orphaned or abandoned infants, including bidoon infants.  Parents were sometimes unable to obtain birth certificates for their bidoon children because of extensive administrative requirements, which prevented such children from accessing public services such as education and health care (see section 2.d., Stateless Persons).

Education:  Education for citizens is free through the university level and compulsory through the secondary level.  Education is neither free nor compulsory for noncitizens.  A 2011 Council of Ministers decree extended education benefits to bidoon.  The government requires Islamic religious instruction in public schools for all students.  The government also requires Islamic religious instruction for Muslim students in private schools that have one or more Muslim students, regardless of whether the student is a citizen or not.  In August 2015 the government allowed 5,000 children of bidoon families to attend public schools.

Medical Care:  Lack of identification papers sometimes restricted bidoon access to public medical care.

Child Abuse:  There was no reported societal pattern of child abuse.  Most cases likely went unreported due to social stigma associated with the disclosure of the practice.  A children's rights law, passed in March 2015 establishing legal protections for abused children, was implemented in January.  In November the government opened a hotline for reporting instances of child abuse.

Early and Forced Marriage:  The legal marriage age is 17 for males and 15 for females, but girls continued to marry at a younger age in some tribal groups.  The government reported there were 3,808 married females between the ages of 15-19.

Sexual Exploitation of Children:  There are no laws specific to child pornography, because all pornography is illegal.  There is no statutory rape law or minimum age for consensual sexual relations, although premarital sexual relations are illegal.

International Child Abductions:  The country is not a party to the 1980 Hague Convention on the Civil Aspects of International Child Abduction.  See the Department of State's *Annual Report on International Parental Child Abduction* at travel.state.gov/content/childabduction/en/legal/compliance.html.

**Anti-Semitism**

There were no known Jewish citizens and an estimated few dozen Jewish foreign resident workers.  Anti-Semitic rhetoric often originated from self-proclaimed Islamists or conservative opinion writers.  These columnists often conflated Israeli government actions or views with those of Jews more broadly.  Reflecting the government's nonrecognition of Israel, there are longstanding official instructions to teachers to expunge from English-language textbooks any references to Israel or the Holocaust.  The law prohibits companies from conducting business with Israeli citizens, including transporting them on their national airlines.

**Trafficking in Persons**

See the Department of State's *Trafficking in Persons Report* at www.state.gov/j/tip/rls/tiprpt/.

**Persons with Disabilities**

The law prohibits discrimination against persons with permanent physical, sensory, intellectual, and mental disabilities, in employment, education, air travel and other transportation, access to health care, or the provision of other government services.

It imposes penalties on employers who refrain without reasonable cause from hiring persons with disabilities.  The law also mandates access to buildings for persons with disabilities.  The government generally enforced these provisions. Noncitizens with disabilities neither had access to government-operated facilities nor received stipends paid to citizens with disabilities that covered transportation, housing, job training, and social welfare costs.  The government still has not fully implemented social and workplace aides for people with physical, and in particular, vision disabilities.

There is a disability law, and a parliamentary Committee for Disabled Affairs. Under that law the monthly allowance given to the mother of a disabled child or the wife of a person with disabilities is 600 dinars ($1,980), and families of citizens with disabilities are eligible to receive grants worth up to 20,000 dinars ($66,000).

During the year the government reserved a small number of admissions to Kuwait University for citizens with disabilities, and there was regular media coverage of students with disabilities attending university classes.  Nonetheless, authorities did not provide noncitizens with disabilities the same educational opportunities, and noncitizen students with disabilities experienced a lack of accessible materials and lack of reasonable accommodations in schools.

Children with disabilities attended public school, but information on whether there were patterns of abuse in educational settings was unavailable.  Representatives from ministries, other governmental bodies, Kuwait University, and several NGOs constituted the government's Higher Council for Handicapped Affairs, which makes policy recommendations; provides direct financial aid to citizens with disabilities; and facilitates their integration into schools, jobs, and other social institutions.  The government supervised and contributed to schools and job training programs oriented to persons with disabilities.

**National/Racial/Ethnic Minorities**

Approximately 70 percent of residents were noncitizens, many originating from Egypt, the Indian subcontinent, and Southeast Asia.  Societal discrimination against noncitizens and bidoon was prevalent and occurred in most areas of daily life, including employment (see section 7.d.), education, housing, social interaction, and health care.  As part of expanded activity against illegal residents, police stopped, arrested, and sometimes deported noncitizens believed to be using private automobiles as taxis.  This action disproportionately affected the noncitizen laborers who could not afford their own automobiles or taxi fares.

**Acts of Violence, Discrimination, and Other Abuses Based on Sexual Orientation and Gender Identity**

Consensual same-sex sexual conduct between men and cross-dressing are illegal. The law punishes consensual same-sex sexual activity between men older than 21 with imprisonment of up of to seven years; those engaging in consensual same-sex sexual activity with men younger than 21 may be imprisoned for as long as 10 years. No laws criminalize sexual behavior between women. The law imposes a fine of 1,059 dinars ($3,495) and imprisonment for one to three years for persons imitating the appearance of the opposite sex in public. Transgender persons reported harassment, detainment, and abuse by security forces.

In August police arrested three cross-dressers in a mall. The police ordered the individuals to have their heads shaved and opened an investigation.

Societal discrimination and harassment based on sexual orientation and gender identity occurred; to a lesser extent, officials also practiced such discrimination, usually upon discovering that a person stopped for a traffic violation did not appear to be the gender indicated on the identification card. Transgender men and women often faced rejection by their families and, in some cases, disputes over inheritances.

No registered NGOs focused on LGBTI matters, although unregistered ones existed. Due to social convention and potential repression, LGBTI organizations neither operated openly nor held gay pride marches or gay rights advocacy events.

**HIV and AIDS Social Stigma**

Local human rights NGOs reported no accounts of societal violence or discrimination against persons with HIV/AIDS, but persons with HIV/AIDS did not generally disclose their status due to social stigma associated with the disease. The Ministry of Health estimated there were 209 citizens with HIV. Foreign citizens found to be HIV-positive faced immediate deportation.

**Other Societal Violence or Discrimination**

Unmarried men continued to face housing discrimination based solely on marital status. The law prohibits single men from obtaining accommodation in many urban residential areas. Single noncitizens faced eviction due to a decision by the municipality to enforce this prohibition and remove them from residences allocated for citizens' families, citing the presence of single men as the reason for increasing crime, a burden on services, and worsening traffic.  Although no law prohibits it, single and unaccompanied citizen and noncitizen female residents traditionally are not allowed to check into hotels.

## Section 7. Worker Rights

### a. Freedom of Association and the Right to Collective Bargaining

The law protects the right of workers to form and join trade unions, bargain collectively, and conduct legal strikes, with significant restrictions.  The government, however, did not always respect these rights.

The law does not apply to public-sector employees, domestic workers, or maritime employees.  Discrete labor laws set work conditions in the public and private sectors, with the oil industry treated separately.  The law permits limited trade union pluralism at the local level, but the government authorized only one federation, the Kuwait Trade Union Federation (KTUF).  The law also stipulates any new union must include at least 100 workers and that at least 15 of the total number must be citizens.

The law provides workers, except for domestic workers, maritime workers, and civil servants, a limited right to collective bargaining.  There is no minimum number of workers needed to conclude such agreements.

Public-sector workers do not have the right to strike.  Private-sector workers have the right to strike, although cumbersome provisions calling for compulsory negotiation and arbitration in the case of disputes limit that right.  The law does not prohibit retaliation against striking workers or prevent the government from interfering in union activities, including the right to strike.

According to the Public Authority for Manpower, there were 2.52 million workers in the country.  Only 19 percent of the total workforce were citizens.  Most citizens (76 percent) worked in the public sector, in part because the government provided lucrative bonuses to citizens, including retirement funding.

The law prohibits antiunion discrimination and employer interference with union functions.  It provides for reinstatement of workers fired for union activity.  Nevertheless, the law empowers the courts to dissolve any union for violating labor laws or for threatening "public order and morals," although a union can appeal such a court decision. The Ministry of Social Affairs and Labor can request the Court of First Instance to dissolve a union. Additionally, the emir may dissolve a union by decree.

Foreign workers, who constituted more than 80 percent of the workforce, may join unions only as nonvoting members after five years of work in the particular sector the union represents, provided they obtain a certificate of good conduct and moral standing from the government. They cannot run for seats or vote in board elections. Both the International Labor Organization and the International Trade Union Confederation criticized the citizenship requirement for discouraging unions in sectors that employ few citizens, including much of private-sector employment, such as construction.

The government enforced applicable laws, with some exceptions, and procedures were generally not subject to lengthy delay or appeals.

The government treated worker actions by citizens and noncitizens differently. While citizens and public sector union leaders and workers faced no government repercussions for their roles in union or strike activities, companies directly threatened noncitizen workers calling for strikes with termination and deportation.

In April, 20,000 Kuwaiti workers in the oil sector went on strike due to proposed future benefit reductions. The strike lasted three days, ending when the government stated it would refuse to negotiate as long as the strike continued. In May, 1,200 foreign oil workers also went on strike due to nonpayment of wages. The government intervened and resolved the strike when it assured the workers they would be paid.

**b. Prohibition of Forced or Compulsory Labor**

The law prohibits and criminally sanctions forced or compulsory labor "except in cases specified by law for national emergency and with just remuneration." In June the National Assembly passed amendments to the private-sector labor law providing for increased worker rights to include subjecting employers to fines for failure to pay worker's wages and for recruiting workers from abroad but failing to provide employment.

Although the law prohibits withholding of workers' passports, the practice remained common among sponsors and employers of foreign workers, and the government demonstrated no consistent efforts to enforce this prohibition. Employers confined some domestic and agricultural workers to their workspaces by retaining their passport and, in the case of some domestic workers, locked in their work locations. Workers who fled abusive employers had difficulty retrieving their passports and authorities deported them in almost all cases. The government usually limited punishment to assessing fines, shutting employment firms, issuing orders for employers to return withheld passports, or requiring employers to pay back wages. As of September the government closed six recruitment agencies and stated it had received and investigated 3,100 complaints from workers, more than half of complaints were resolved amicably in favor of the worker. The government also received 9,087 salary-related labor complaints, of which 6,123 were referred to the labor courts for adjudication while 463 cases were resolved through arbitration.

Some incidents of forced labor and conditions indicative of forced labor occurred, especially among foreign domestic and agricultural workers. Such practices were usually a result of employer abuse of the sponsorship system (kafala) for noncitizen workers. Employers frequently illegally withheld salaries from domestic workers and minimum-wage laborers.

According to various reports, North Korean laborers, estimated to number between 2,000 and 4,000, worked in forced labor conditions, averaging 15-hour days with no freedom of movement and living in squalid conditions. Former North Korean laborers and officials indicated that employers paid worker salaries to a North Korean government-owned company instead of directly to the individual workers. Kuwait served as the only point of aerial disembarkation for all North Korean laborers in Gulf Cooperation Council countries. In October the government halted all North Korean flights to Kuwait in response to repeated requests from concerned governments, and in November the government ceased issuing work visas for North Korean workers.

Domestic servitude was the most common type of forced labor, principally involving foreign domestic workers employed under the sponsorship system, but reports of forced labor in the construction and sanitation sectors also existed. Forced labor conditions for migrant workers included nonpayment of wages, long working hours, deprivation of food, threats, physical and sexual abuse, and restrictions on movement, such as withholding passports or confinement to the workplace. As of September employers filed 18,385 "absconding" reports against employees versus 37 complaints filed by domestic workers against their employers in accordance with the new domestic labor law.

The Public Authority for Manpower operated a shelter for abused domestic workers, and as of July, according to a government source, the shelter had a capacity of 500 victims and housed on average 350 at any one time.  International and national organizations had relatively open access to workers residing in the shelter and reported adequate living conditions.  After observers accused male guards of abusing and sexually harassing some of the women, the shelter modified security arrangements to forbid male security guards from entering the operating and lodging areas of the shelter.

In July the government began implementing the 2015 domestic worker labor law that requires employers to grant domestic workers a maximum 12-hour workday, with one day off per week and 30 days paid leave per year.  The law also establishes a minimum wage of 60 dinars ($198), end-of-service benefits--one month's wage for every year worked--and bans employing domestic workers below age 20 or more than 50 years of age.  Parliament also voted in 2015 to establish a shareholding company for recruiting domestic workers.  The law went into effect in May, and the board of the shareholding company was established in November.  The government regularly conducted information awareness campaigns via media outlets and public events, and otherwise informed employers, in order to encourage compliance by the public and private recruiting companies with the new law.

There were numerous media reports throughout the year of sponsors abusing domestic workers or significantly injuring them while they tried to escape; some reports alleged abuse resulted in workers' deaths.  Female domestic workers were particularly vulnerable to sexual abuse.  Police and courts were reluctant to prosecute citizens for abuse in private residences but prosecuted serious cases of abuse when reported.  According to a high-level government official, authorities prosecuted several cases of domestic worker abuse.  At year's end a female citizen was serving a 10-year prison term for abusing a domestic worker.  In December 2015 an appeals court overruled a lower court's acquittal of a female citizen for assaulting her domestic worker.  In February the Court of Cassation upheld the appeals court verdict, and the citizen was sentenced to three and one-half years in prison.

Numerous media reports highlighted the problem of visa trading and human rights.  Arrests of visa traffickers and illegal labor rings occurred almost weekly.  Since workers cannot freely change jobs, they were sometimes willing to leave their initial job due to low wages or unacceptable working conditions and enter into an illegal residency status with the hope of improved working conditions at another job.  As of August the public prosecutor's office had referred 606 recruiting firms for prosecution for illegal issuance of residency permits.

See also the Department of State's *Trafficking in Persons Report* at www.state.gov/j/tip/rls/tiprpt/.

## c. Prohibition of Child Labor and Minimum Age for Employment

The law prohibits child labor.  The legal minimum age for employment is 18, although employers may obtain permits from the Ministry of Social Affairs and Labor to employ juveniles between 15 and 18 in some nonhazardous trades. Juveniles may work a maximum of six hours a day with no more than four consecutive hours followed by a one-hour rest period.  Juveniles cannot work overtime or between 7 p.m. and 6 a.m.

Although not extensive, there were credible reports that children of South Asian origin worked as domestic laborers.  Some underage workers entered the country on travel documents with falsified birth dates.

The government made efforts to enforce laws regulating child labor. Approximately 450 Ministry of Social Affairs and Labor inspectors routinely monitored private firms for labor law compliance, including laws against child labor.  Noncompliant employers faced fines or a forced suspension of their company operations.  Nevertheless, the government did not consistently enforce child labor laws in the informal sector, such as in street vending.

## d. Discrimination with Respect for Employment and Occupation

The law prohibits discrimination in employment based on race, sex, gender, and disability.  The government immediately deports HIV-positive foreign workers, and there is no protection for workers based on sexual orientation.  No laws prohibit labor discrimination based on language, non-HIV communicable diseases, or social status, but there were no reported cases of discrimination in these areas.

Discrimination in employment and occupation occurred with respect to both citizen and noncitizen women.  Domestic workers were at particular risk of discrimination or abuse due to the isolated home environment in which they worked.  Shia continued to report government discrimination based on religion. For example, Shia were represented in police force and military/security apparatus, although not in all branches and often not in leadership positions.  Some Shia continued to allege that a glass ceiling of discrimination prevented them from obtaining leadership positions in public-sector organizations, including the security services.  In the private sector, Shia were generally represented at all levels in proportion to their percentage of the population.

The law states that a woman should receive "remuneration equal to that of a man provided she does the same work," although it prohibits women from working in "dangerous industries" and in trades "harmful" to health.  Educated women contended the conservative nature of society restricted career opportunities, although there were limited improvements.  While women were 72 percent of college graduates from Kuwait University, they were underrepresented in the number of students sent to study internationally, likely due to continued societal concerns about permitting young women to study away from their families.  Prior to an October court ruling, female medical school applicants were required to demonstrate a higher minimum grade point average than male applicants.  According to government statistics, the female workforce participation rate was 58 percent while according to the World Bank the percentage of women in the workforce was 45 percent.

**e. Acceptable Conditions of Work**

The law sets the national minimum wage in the private sector at 65 dinars ($215) per month.  The actual minimum wage for domestic workers was 60 dinars ($198) per month.  Most low-wage employees lived and worked in the country without their families, and employers provided at least some form of housing.

The law limits the standard workweek to 48 hours (40 hours for the petroleum industry), and gives private-sector workers 30 days of annual leave.  The law also forbids requiring employees to work more than 60 hours per week or 10 hours per day.  The law provides for 13 designated national holidays annually.  Workers are entitled to 125 percent of base pay for working overtime and 150 percent of base pay for working on their designated weekly day off.

The government issued occupational health and safety standards that were current and appropriate for the main industries.  For example, the law provides that all outdoor work stop between 11 a.m. and 4 p.m. during June, July, and August, or when the temperature rises to more than 120 degrees Fahrenheit in the shade.  A worker could file a complaint against an employer with the Public Authority for Manpower if the worker believed his safety and health were at risk.

The law and regulations governing acceptable conditions of work do not apply to domestic workers. The Ministry of Interior has jurisdiction over domestic worker matters and enforces domestic labor working standards via the new domestic labor law that was implemented in July.

The Ministry of Social Affairs and Labor is responsible for enforcement of wage and hours, overtime, and occupational safety and health regulations of nondomestic workers. Enforcement by the ministry was generally good, but there were gaps in enforcement with respect to unskilled foreign laborers. Several ministry officials cited inadequate numbers of inspectors as the main reason for their inability to enforce the laws to the best of their abilities.

Approximately 450 labor inspectors monitored private firms. The government periodically inspected enterprises to raise awareness among workers and employers and to assure that they abided by existing safety rules, controlled pollution in certain industries, trained workers to use machines, and reported violations.

The Ministry of Social Affairs and Labor monitored worksites to provide for compliance with rules banning summer work and recorded hundreds of violations during the year. Workers could also report these violations to their embassies, the KTUF, or the Labor Disputes Department. Noncompliant employers faced warnings, fines, or forced suspensions of company operations, but these were not sufficiently substantial to deter violators.

Workers submitted complaints to the Public Authority for Manpower Labor Relations. In the first 10 months of the year, the Labor Disputes Department received 12,187 complaints from workers; these complaints were either about contract issues such as nonpayment of wages or about difficulties transferring work visas to new companies. Most of the complaints were resolved in arbitration, with the remaining cases referred to the courts for resolution.

At times the Public Authority for Manpower intervened to resolve labor disputes between foreign workers and their employers. The authority's labor arbitration panel sometimes ruled in favor of foreign laborers who claimed violations of work contracts by their employers. The government was more effective in resolving unpaid salary disputes involving private sector laborers than those involving domestic workers.

Foreign workers were vulnerable to unacceptable conditions of work. Domestic workers and other unskilled foreign workers in the private sector frequently worked substantially in excess of 48 hours a week, with no day of rest.

Domestic workers had little recourse when employers violated their rights except to seek admittance to the domestic workers shelter where the government mediated between sponsors and workers either to assist the worker in finding an alternate sponsor or to assist in voluntary repatriation. There were no inspections of private residences, the workplace of the majority of the country's domestic workers. Reports indicated employers forced domestic workers to work overtime without additional compensation.

Some domestic workers did not have the ability to remove themselves from an unhealthy or unsafe situation without endangering their employment. There were reports of domestic workers' committing or attempting to commit suicide due to desperation over abuse, including sexual violence, or poor working conditions. In July, the government implemented the domestic labor law (68/2015) that provides legal protections for domestic workers for the first time. The law establishes a formal grievance process and identifies the Domestic Labor Department at the Ministry of Interior as the sole arbitration entity for domestic worker labor disputes. A worker not satisfied with the department's arbitration decision has the right to file a legal case via the labor court. As of November the department had conducted 1,387 inspections of domestic worker recruiting agencies and closed 76 of them for failing to meet the requirements of the new law.

Several embassies with large domestic worker populations in the country met with varying degrees of success in pressing the government to prosecute serious cases of domestic worker abuse. Severe cases included those where there were significant, life-threatening injuries.